♥

"I WANT YOU TO ALWAYS KNOW HOW MUCH I APPRECIATE YOU AND OUR FRIENDSHIP"
—Susan Polis Schutz

♥

FIND A GOOD FRIEND . . . BE A TRUE FRIEND . . . REAP THE SUBLIME JOYS OF FRIENDSHIP!

♥

"One picks up Susan's poetry and reads it to the quiet
and tasteful accompaniment of Stephen's art and suddenly you
are with friends you want to know and to
speak with more."
—Saturday Evening Post

♥

"A poet of the heart."
—Family Weekly

♥

"In high emotion . . . the reigning star is
Susan Polis Schutz."
—Time

♥

"Susan Polis Schutz remains one of the most popular poets in
America today, and her work touches
virtually everyone."
—Associated Press

♥

"Susan Polis Schutz's popularity can be attributed to her ability
to verbalize intimate, honest emotions shared but unsaid by
most people. Her ability to write simply and honestly of the
deepest emotions and the most fragile and fleeting of moments
strikes a responsive chord with readers."
—Woman's Day

♥

"Susan's work continues to touch the hearts of millions across
the world, sharing patience and joy, peace and
love with people everywhere . . . "
—True Story

♥

Books by Susan Polis Schutz

♥

To My Son With Love

To My Daughter With Love

I Love You

♥

Also edited by Susan Polis Schutz

♥

To My Father With Love

Mother, I Will Always Love You

Don't Ever Stop Dreaming Your Dreams

♥

Published by
WARNER BOOKS

A Friend Is Forever

A Collection of Poems
Edited by Susan Polis Schutz

WARNER BOOKS

A Time Warner Company

Warner Books, Inc., 1271 Avenue of the Americas, New York, NY 10020

 A Time Warner Company

Printed in the United States of America

First Warner Books Printing: May 1993

10 9 8 7 6 5 4 3 2

Library of Congress Cataloging-in-Publication Data

A Friend is forever : a collection of poems / edited by Susan Polis
Schutz.
    p.   cm.
  ISBN 0–446–39318–5
  1. Friendship--Poetry.   2. American poetry.   I. Schutz, Susan
Polis.
PS595.F75F74 1993
811.008 ' 0353--dc20   92-37133
                                                          CIP

CONTENTS

You Will Always Be
My Friend

Sometime ago
I received a special gift,
and it came in the form of you,
   my friend.
You are so important to me,
   and I want to thank you
      for all the wonderful memories.
Whenever I see you,
   I am reminded of myself.
Whenever I think of you, I am reminded
   of all the good times we've had.
Together we've done so much,
   seen so much, and felt so much.
With a knowing smile,
I look back at the shared times
   and all the things only you and I know.
With high hopes and great expectations,
I look ahead to the future
   and all the things only you and I
      will share.
You not only put a smile on my face;
   you put a smile in my heart.
You will always be my friend.

—Barbara Iantosca

Some Friends Are Forever

Sometimes in life,
you find a special friend;
someone who changes your life
by being a part of it.
Someone who makes you laugh
until you can't stop;
someone who makes you believe
that there really is good in the world.
Someone who convinces you
that there is an unlocked door
just waiting for you to open it.
This is forever friendship.

When you're down,
and the world seems dark and empty,
your forever friend lifts you up in spirit
and makes that dark and empty world
suddenly seem bright and full.
Your forever friend gets you through
the hard times, the sad times,
and the confused times.
If you turn and walk away,
your forever friend follows.
If you lose your way,
your forever friend guides you
and cheers you on.
Your forever friend holds your hand
and tells you that
everything is going to be okay.
And if you find such a friend,
you feel happy and complete,
because you need not worry.
You have a forever friend for life,
and forever has no end.

—Laurieann Kelly

You Are a Perfect Friend

You have known me
in good and
bad times
You have seen me
when I was happy
and when I was sad
You have listened to me
when what I said was intelligent
and when I talked nonsense
You have been with me
when we had fun
and when we were miserable
You have watched me
laugh
and cry
You have understood me
when I knew what I was doing
and when I made mistakes
Thank you for
believing in me
for supporting me
and for always being ready
to share thoughts together
You are a perfect friend

—Susan Polis Schutz

To My Very
Good Friend

We have all had many friends
throughout our lives,
but only a few of those friends
we would call good friends.
That's because being a good friend
involves time
and understanding
and love,
which can be difficult to share
with another.
When I think of my good friends,
I always think about you,
because that is what you have
   been to me.

You have taken the time
to be there when I needed you,
and you have listened to me
when my life was changing.
You have always cared enough
to try to understand my feelings
and help me to understand myself.
And, most important,
your consideration and honesty
have shown me
that your friendship is true . . .
symbolizing a very special kind
    of love
that only a few friends
ever share with one another.
Thank you for being such
a good friend to me,
and for all the joys we have known
together.

—Laura Medley

Thanks for Being
My Friend

I want to tell you that
your friendship has been such
a blessing to my life,
and I am thankful beyond words
for having someone to confide in,
someone who overlooks my faults
    and shortcomings,
and focuses on my strengths.

I realize how fortunate I am to have
you to praise my triumphs
and soothe my sorrows.
We both know that life brings
joy and sometimes pain,
and when there's a special friend
to share it with,
the good times are better
and the bad ones aren't so bad.

For you, for your life,
and for your friendship,
I give thanks to you,
my dearest friend.

—Shelby Lewis Jones

A Friend
Is One of Life's
Most Beautiful Gifts

A friend is a person you can trust,
who won't turn away from you;
a friend will be there
when you really need someone,
and will come to you
when they need help.
A friend will listen to you
even when they don't understand
or agree with your feelings;
a friend will never try
to change you,
but appreciates you for who you are.
A friend doesn't expect too much
or give too little;
a friend is someone you can share
dreams, hopes, and fears with.

A friend is a person you can think of
and suddenly smile;
a friend doesn't have to be told
that they are special,
because they know you feel that way.
A friend will accept your attitudes,
ideas, and emotions,
even when their own are different,
and will hold your hand
when you're scared.
A friend will be honest with you
even when it might hurt,
and will forgive you
for the mistakes you make.
A friend can never disappoint you,
and will support you
and share in your glory.
A friend shares responsibility
when you have doubts.
A friend always remembers
the little things you've done,
the times you've shared,
and the talks you've had.
A friend will bend over backwards
to help you pick up the pieces
when your world falls apart.
A friend is one of life's
most beautiful gifts.

—Luann Auciello

My Friend . . .

You are the most significant person in my life right now. You are my dearest friend, the one person I can be open and honest with, the person who knows me better than I know myself and still loves me. When I am with you, I am able to strip away the masks and stop all the game-playing. I can be myself, with no pretense, and I am accepted and loved completely for who I am. There are no surprises with you; I know who you are, and you know who I am, and we are able to love one another completely.

We aren't always able to spend as much time together as we'd like, but when we are together, it's as if we had never been apart. Being with you makes me laugh, and it gives me a safe place to cry. You are sensitive and bright and an altogether lovely companion.

I love you for being the wonderful person that you are and for the beauty you bring into my life just by being there. I love you for listening to all my troubles and for sharing yours with me. I love you for your acceptance of me, even when you don't agree with my actions or decisions. I love you for the fun we have together and the openness that characterizes our relationship. I love you most of all for being a terrific person and the best friend anyone could have.

—Donna Taylor

You Are Someone Special
Who Has Made All the Difference
in My Life

You are different from anyone
I've ever met before.
And yet, somehow, there's
something distinctly familiar
about you.
Maybe it's in the way
your eyes laugh so clearly
or maybe it has something to do
with the warmth in your heart.
Whatever it is, it's the reflection
of your beautiful soul.

There was a time when
I'd given up on the world —
I was determined not to be
    a part of it,
because I'd never known anyone
to understand or care like you do.
I've been through changes,
both good and bad,
and I've come to appreciate
the world's beautiful people
who keep alive laughter,
love, and hope.
You have a great gift,
and that gift is yourself.
I'd like to thank you
for choosing to share
that gift with me.
And though no one person
may be able to change the world,
I want you to know that,
at least in one life,
you have made
a significant difference.

—Grace F. Jacoby

Year after year,
we see ourselves change,
and the world changes around us.
We are never the same
from day to day,
and we experience life
in so many ways.
At times, it challenges us
with unexpected difficulties,
but we become stronger
and more self-sufficient;
we learn how to depend on ourselves
and rely on one another.

As friends,
we have come to understand
that even if life
is not always perfect,
when we have each other
to enjoy the better moments,
it doesn't have to be perfect
to be special.

—Laura Medley

When two people are as close
as we are,
there isn't any need
to tell each other
that we are the best of friends.
There's a bond present between us
that has gradually strengthened
throughout the years,
whether we are close together
or miles apart.
I can't say that
we haven't had any quarrels
or faced any hardships,
because we have.
But through them
we have realized just how precious
our relationship is to us
and how essential it is to our lives.

You have graciously
shared your love with me,
which is the most any individual
can offer another person.
It's very important to me now
that I let you know
how beautiful my life is
with you in it,
and because we are so close,
I simply want to remind you
that you truly are
my best friend.

—Mary Renée Kunz

My Friend,
I Have So Many Wishes for You

I wish for you to have
people to love
people in your life who will care about you
as much as I do
blue skies and clear days
exciting things to do
easy solutions to any problems
knowledge to make the right decisions
strength in your values
laughter and fun
goals to pursue
happiness in all that you do
I wish for you to have
beautiful experiences
each new day
as you follow
your dreams

—Susan Polis Schutz

You Are
the Friend
I Will Cherish Forever

Once in a long while,
someone special walks into your life
and really makes a difference.
They take the time
to show you in so many little ways
that you matter.
They see and hear the worst in you,
the ugliest in you,
but they don't walk away;
in fact, they may care more about you.
Their heart breaks with yours,
their tears fall with yours,
their laughter is shared with yours.

Once in a long while,
somebody special walks into your life
and then has to go their separate way.
Every time you see a certain gesture,
hear a certain laugh or phrase,
or return to a certain place,
it reminds you of them.
You treasure the time you had with them;
your eyes fill with tears,
a big smile comes across your face,
and you thank God that someone
can still touch your heart so deeply.
You remember their words, their looks,
their expressions;
you remember how much of themselves
they gave — not just to you,
but to all.
You remember the strength
that amazed you,
the courage that impressed you,
the grace that inspired you,
and the love that touched you.

—Laurie Winkelmann

What could be sweeter
than a friend who doesn't mind
listening to your troubles —
one who's always interested
   in what you think
and what's going on in your life?

What could be more precious
than a friend who always reassures you
that you are special —
a friend who makes you feel like you mean
   so much to them?

What could be more wished for
than a friend who knows
how to help you forget your problems —
who can turn your insecurities and your tears
into self-assurance and laughter?

You are the friend I always hoped I'd find,
and your friendship is invaluable to me.

—Karen Doede

"The Friendship Poem"

Friends do things for one another. They understand.
They go a million miles out of their way.
They hold your hand. They bring you smiles,
when a smile is exactly what you needed.
They listen, and they hear what is said
in the spaces between the words. They care.
And they let you know you're in their prayers.

Friends always know the perfect thing to do.
They can make your whole day just by saying
something that no one else could have said.
Sometimes you feel like the two of you share
a secret language that others can't tune into.

A friend can guide you, inspire you, comfort you, or light up your life with laughter. A friend understands your moods and nurtures your needs. A friend lovingly knows just what you're after.

When your feelings come from deep inside and they need to be spoken to someone you don't have to hide from, you share them . . . with a friend. When good news comes, a friend is the first one you turn to. When feelings overflow and tears need to fall, friends help you through it all.

Friends bring sunlight into your life. They warm your life with their presence, whether they are far away or close by your side. A friend is a gift that brings happiness, and a treasure that money can't buy.

—Collin McCarty

For a Very Special Friend

There are so many things
to do each day
There is so much going on in the world
of great concern
that often we do not stop and think about
what is really important to us
One of the nicest things in my life
is my friendship with you
and even if we don't have a lot of time
to spend with each other
I want you to always know
how much I appreciate you
and our friendship

—Susan Polis Schutz

I Could Never Have
a Better Friend than You

How do I thank you for what
   you've given me,
when it comes so naturally for you
to be so loving and such a great friend?
It takes no effort for you to be sincere,
   honest, and straightforward.
It's easy for you to be crazy,
   fun, and humorous.
Your understanding ear and warm hugs,
your accepting and reassuring smile —
   they're a part of you.

The good times we share,
   the talks,
the problems we solve together,
the aspects of me that only you
   can comprehend —
they prove to me again and again
what a special friend you are!
They make it clear to me
that no one can match you as a friend.

—Linda C. Alderman

You're a very special friend to me.

And I really cherish
    all the wonderful qualities you have:
    the ones that shine so brightly for everyone to see
and the more personal ones . . . that are
    only known to the lucky people
        who are close to you.

You've got so many good things going for you.
    And the more I know of this world
        and of the people in it,
the more I know that you're really one of a kind.

I think I could search the world over and never
    find a more wonderful friend than you.

—Chris Gallatin

Once in a while a special friend
comes into your life
and touches you in a wonderful way.
Your personalities just seem to click,
and it seems as though your friendship
has existed for years.
Immediately there is a sense
of trust and sincerity,
and a feeling of closeness
develops instantly.
It's refreshing not to have
    the usual barriers to overcome,
and right away you know
you have found a friend.
Even after parting,
this person leaves such an impression
that from time to time, for no reason,
you think of that friend,
    and it makes you happy.
I'm really lucky,
because somebody special
came into my life
and touched me in that magical way.
And it just so happens
that somebody is you.
Thanks for the magic!

—Brenda Neville

Our Friendship Is the Best

A good friendship
doesn't demand anything,
but accepts whatever time
there is to be together.
It doesn't expect everything
to be perfect,
but values the kindness
and sincerity
that is shared when friends
trust one another.
A good friendship
is a relationship in which
two people understand
their differences
and respect their uniqueness.
They allow each other to be
exactly who they are,
and enjoy the discovery
of themselves.
A good friendship
is exactly what we have,
and I thought you should know
that I think you are one of
the best friends
anyone could ever have.

—Deanna Beisser

Friendship is more
than just having someone
to talk to and laugh with.
It is listening.
It is taking a chance
and sharing a part of yourself
with someone else.
It is sometimes giving
much more than you are getting
but being thankful
that you are there
to help your friend.

Friendship is the belief
that someone else's happiness
is important to your own.
It is knowing that this person
represents something special,
something to be treasured for a lifetime.
You have taught me
all this and more,
simply by being my friend.

—Christine McCarthy

I Don't Know What
I Would Do Without You

I know that I can always
come to you with anything —
a problem I'm struggling with,
a decision I'm trying to work out,
a hurt or a joy,
or just to let off steam.
Your serenity calms me,
your compassion comforts me,
your wisdom counsels me,
and your love sustains me.

No matter what it is,
you let me talk it out for myself
and give me honest advice
when I ask for it.
You never judge me,
and you never preach to me.
You just accept me as I am,
for what I am and who I am
at this particular time in my life.
You don't try to change me.
You give me credit
for the growth in my life
and believe in me
for the growing I have left to do.
Thanks for being there,
    for listening,
        and for being my friend.

—Sandy Harshberger

You Are Always
My Friend

You are always
   my friend
when I am happy
or when I am sad
when I am all alone
or when I am with people
You are always my friend
if I see you today
or if I see you
   a year from now
if I talk to you today
or if I talk to you
   a year from now
You are always my friend
   and though through the years
we will change
it does not matter what I do
or it does not matter what you do
Throughout our lifetime
you are always my friend

—Susan Polis Schutz

Our Friendship
Means Everything
in the World to Me

Our friendship means that I have someone
who will drop whatever they're doing
to be with me when I need them.
It means that I have someone I
can trust with my most intimate
secrets and thoughts.

Our friendship means that there's
someone I can count on to listen
to my problems and complaints
without judging me.
It means that someone really knows
and understands me
and loves me anyway.

Our friendship means
that I have a person in my life
who believes in my hopes and dreams
and encourages me to fulfill them.
It means that I have someone
with whom I can share laughter, hugs,
and special times.

Our friendship means
that there is someone in this world
who is completely irreplaceable in my life,
who is a loving heart, a companion,
    a confidant.
It means that I am among
the lucky few who have a friend
who is part of their very soul.
I have a friend who is
a special, unique,
and essential part of myself:
you.

—Barbara Cage

I can't even begin to tell you
how much it's meant to me
to have you as a friend.

There are lots of times when
    I don't know what I'd do without you.
There are times when my sun
    forgets to shine, and you brighten
    up my life in a way that
        nobody else knows how to.
There are feelings I can share with you
    and discussions we can have
    that I wouldn't feel comfortable
    sharing with anyone else.
There are just so many nice things you
    bring to my life . . . and so many
        reasons why I'm glad you're here.

—Carey Martin

I have always seen my life
as a journey on a road
to tomorrow.
There have been hills and valleys
and turns here and there
that have filled my life with
all kinds of challenges and changes.
But I made it through those times,
because there were always
special friends I met
along the way.

My special friends
are the ones who
have walked beside me,
comforting my spirit or
holding my hand
when I needed it the most.
They were friends who
loved my smiles
and were not afraid of my tears.
They were true friends
who really cared about me.
Those friends are forever;
they are cherished and loved
more than they'll ever know.

—Deanna Beisser

Thank You, My Friend,
for All that You Are to Me

You are my friend.
You know me better
    and understand me more
        than anyone else.
Yet sometimes I forget to say thanks.
I know it's not always easy
    being my friend.
Sometimes I lean too much
or say the wrong thing.
Other times I'm out-of-sorts
and just not the best company.
But it doesn't seem to matter.
You still stick by me,
and that makes you very special.
If I forget to say thanks
or don't tell you
    how much you mean to me,
please know I couldn't make it
    without you.
And I wouldn't want to try.

—Julia Baron Alvarez

The Essence of
Lifelong Friendship

A lifelong friend
is one who enters your life
at a time when they are needed most.
Though you may not understand it,
there will be an instant bonding
between you
and a realization
that this person was brought to you,
not only to fill an emptiness
or assist you in time of need,
but to form an eternal friendship.

A lifelong friend
is a friend who knows you like no other,
who is so much a part of you
that distance does not cause separation.
They will hurt when you hurt,
and feel joy when you are joyous.
They know your imperfections
and they accept them as a part of you.
Though they may not
agree with your decisions,
they will support you completely
in everything you do.
They respect you and your right
to make your life what you want it to be.
When all the others have come and gone,
this friend will be with you;
even if your world falls apart,
they will be there to build it back up
better and stronger than before.
This is the essence of lifelong friendship.

—Lisa VanEllen

True Friends

There are many people
that we meet in our lives
but only a very few
will make a lasting impression
on our minds and hearts
It is these people that we will
think of often
and who will always remain
important to us
as true friends

—Susan Polis Schutz

You Are One
of the Best Friends
I've Ever Known

You are my friend.
You listen to what I have to say,
no matter how trivial,
no matter how unimportant.
You listen without judging;
you give your opinion when asked.
You listen wholeheartedly,
without distractions.

You care about me,
about who I am,
where I am going,
what I am doing.
You care about our relationship
and make that extra effort
to make me feel at home with you.

We complement and complete
    each other.
You give so much of yourself
to me and to others,
without ever expecting
    more in return.

You are my friend,
and you'll always be
a part of my life.

—Barbara Carlson

ACKNOWLEDGMENTS

The following is a partial list of authors whom the publisher especially wishes to thank for permission to reprint their works.

Linda C. Alderman for "I Could Never Have a Better Friend than You." Copyright © 1992 by Linda C. Alderman. All rights reserved. Reprinted by permission.

Deanna Beisser for "Our Friendship Is the Best." Copyright © 1992 by Deanna Beisser. All rights reserved. Reprinted by permission.

Sandy Harshberger for "I Don't Know What I Would Do Without You." Copyright © 1992 by Sandy Harshberger. All rights reserved. Reprinted by permission.

Christine McCarthy for "Friendship is more . . ." Copyright © 1992 by Christine McCarthy. All rights reserved. Reprinted by permission.